The Management Guide to Motivating

Kate Keenan

RAVETTE PUBLISHING

Published by Ravette Publishing Limited
P.O. Box 296
Horsham
West Sussex RH13 8FH

Telephone: (01403) 711443
Fax: (01403) 711554

First printed 1995
Reprinted 1997

Series Editor – Anne Tauté
Editor – Catriona Scott

Cover design – Jim Wire
Printing & Binding – Cox & Wyman Ltd.
Production – Oval Projects Ltd.

An Oval Project
for Ravette Publishing.

Cover – Newton's cradle: For every action
there is an equal and opposite reaction.

Acknowledgments and thanks to:
Barry Tuckwood
Jeremy Bethell

Contents

This book is dedicated to
those who would like to manage better
but are too busy to begin.

Motivating

The concept of motivation is often seen as a mystery – a commodity something akin to magic dust which you sprinkle over people and suddenly everyone is full of energy and a willingness to work productively.

In fact, the concept of motivation is remarkably simple. It has to do with how individuals are treated and how good they feel about what they are doing.

But what you have to do to get people motivated, and then to keep them that way, is not quite so easy. This book helps you understand the nature of motivation and gives practical suggestions as to how to go about creating highly motivated people and sustaining their momentum.

1.   The Need for Motivating

Motivating is a vital aspect of working well. It has to do with how committed people are to doing their work and achieving their goals, even if these are as simple as the wish to make more money or go home early.

Signs of Low Morale

Recognizing that people are not motivated is not as simple as it sounds. They do not always tell you how they are feeling or admit that they are dissatisfied, but they can often show signs of not being happy with their lot. If things are going well there is usually an atmosphere of energy and interest which you can sense. If this is absent, it should alert you straight away.

Discontent will also be reflected in general behaviour and some of the signs to look out for are:

- Not co-operating when extra effort is needed.
- Being reluctant to volunteer to do extra things.
- Arriving late, leaving early, or taking a day off without a satisfactory explanation.
- Dragging out tea-breaks and mealtimes to get the maximum amount of time off work.
- Missing deadlines because the task has not been completed on time.

- Not measuring up to standards.
- Complaining constantly about trivial things.
- Blaming others when things are not working well.
- Neglecting to follow instructions.

The presence of just one of these negative aspects does not necessarily mean that people are demotivated, but a combination of two or three should make warning bells ring.

People's behaviour may be telling you something about the situation in which they are working or the way they are being managed. You need to find out what is causing their demoralization and work out what would motivate people to improve.

Reacting Negatively

When things are not going as well as they should be, people will often express attitudes which indicate that they are not happy. Here are some classic phrases with which these feelings can be vented:

- **"It should never have happened"**: spending time apportioning the blame for the current mess, rather than solving the problem.

- **"If only they'd listened to us"**: harping back to the past and mulling over failures.

- **"What a company to work for"**: probably the most self-defeating attitude of all – if it is such a lousy company, why are people still there?

- **"I'm always the last to know"**: indicating that communication is not working properly, or is non-existent.

- **"It's all their fault"**: blaming a nebulous group of others and thus distancing personal responsibility.

- **"So what's new?"**: grudgingly accepting the situation without being prepared to do anything about it.

- **"Who cares anyway?"**: abdicating personal responsibility for producing poor work.

- **"I might have known that would happen"**: indicating that there is no expectation of high standards or good work.

- **"Nobody ever tells me anything"**: not taking the initiative to find out what is happening.

All these responses point to underlying negative attitudes. These are all too readily communicated to others. Unwittingly, the few who are themselves demoralized can demotivate a large number of people incredibly easily – and once people are demotivated, it is much more difficult to restore morale and improve productivity.

Performing Poorly

It is easy to attribute poor performance to a lack of motivation. In reality there are a number of reasons why this may occur, none of which may have anything to do with individual motivation. The factors which prevent good performance might be:

- **Insufficient training**. If there have been substantial changes to the job, people may not be as competent as they were and therefore more reluctant to make an effort. Or it may be that relevant training has not been provided from the start.

- **Incompetence**. If people are not competent in their jobs, you may get the impression that they are lazy. Few people are prepared to admit that they lack knowledge or ability; they will usually prefer to produce excuses as to why the work cannot be done.

- **Weak discipline**. If disciplinary procedures are rarely used to the limit, this can cause people to hold a cynical attitude to work.

- **Low standards**. If the standards to which a task is required to conform have not been clearly defined, it could seem to the person doing the work that "Whatever I do, it's wrong".

- **Poor management**. If people have been badly managed in the past, they may have little respect for control of any sort. They will do what they are told to do, but their responses may not be enthusiastic.

- **Personal problems**. If a substantial change in an individual's attitude occurs, it may signal that domestic difficulties have become insurmountable.

Misunderstanding Motivation

Understanding what motivates individuals can be puzzling. When asked to identify what motivates other people, it is tempting to give as reasons those things which motivate you, mistakenly assuming that others react in exactly the same way as you would in the circumstances. For example, you may be prepared to make an extra effort for any of these motives:

- Being able to achieve things and see the results from personal effort.
- Having the freedom to do things in an individual way.
- Having responsibility.

All these reasons are based on the opportunity for personal achievement and recognition. But if you find these are not the things that motivate someone else, it may be difficult for you to identify those that are.

On the other hand, it is often a mistake to think that other people could be motivated by less complex objectives than your own; you may be underestimating their aspirations. The most common mistaken beliefs are that:

● They just work for the money.
● They need the security of the job.
● They like being with other people and being supported by the group.

These elements may motivate some people some of the time, but they certainly will not motivate all people all the time. Nor are they the only things; there are many other factors, including basic ones, which need to be understood.

Summary: Identifying Demotivation

Demotivation is insidious. It is like having toothache: not life-threatening, but debilitating. Being able to spot that people are not happy in what they are doing is a prerequisite for motivating them.

Addressing the reasons for poor performance and working to eliminate negative attitudes, as well as understanding individual needs, are all key components in the process of motivating people to work better.

Questions to Ask Yourself

Think about the people with whom you work and ask yourself the following questions:

♦ Are people unwilling to make an extra effort?

♦ Are they constantly moaning?

♦ Are they never there when I need them?

♦ Do they always blame others, possibly me, when things go wrong?

♦ Have there been any substantial changes to the work environment or the business itself?

♦ Are people finding their work more difficult than previously?

♦ Do I tend to misunderstand what motivates them?

If you answer 'Yes' to all or any of these questions, it is likely that you have some cause for concern as to how motivated people are.

You Will Be Doing Better If...

★ You can recognize whether people are not as motivated as you would like them to be.

★ You can identify any aspects which may be causing demotivation.

★ You can diagnose the possible reasons for this.

★ You can recognize negative reactions and an atmosphere which indicates that all is not well.

★ You are able to distinguish where poor performance may be due to factors other than demotivation.

★ You realize that it is easy to misunderstand what motivates other people.

2. Understanding Basic Needs

To understand what motivates people, you need to appreciate that people have a number of basic needs that drive them to thrive and prosper.

The Driving Forces

There are three fundamental areas in life that people require to satisfy. These can be viewed as three levels which together form a hierarchy of needs.

Level 1: Basic Requirements

The basic needs – food, water and warmth – require to be satisfied if you are to survive. These needs cannot be ignored nor wished away.

If you were out in the wild you would need to hunt and fish to feed yourself. In a mostly urban society this need is converted to earning a living to supply the necessities. In most societies, money is the medium through which these needs are satisfied. It provides the wherewithal to assuage hunger, thirst and cold.

But money alone can never provide total motivation. Salary or wages act as motivators only in that they provide the answer to the question, "Why work?"

Many people think that the more you pay people,

the more they will be motivated. However, money can only really motivate people to get out of bed and go to work. Provided the payment hovers around the accepted level for the job, money itself tends to have very little effect in getting people to produce sustained extra effort. To increase the amount of money paid for the job will not necessarily make them want to work better. For example, a pay rise of £50 a week will soon be absorbed into normal living costs and people will wonder how on earth they managed before.

Once the basic drives are satisfied through earning enough money to provide what is essential, it is the higher level needs which begin to make themselves felt.

Level 2: Social Status

People need to feel that they belong. They work to acquire a definite place in their society. Social needs differ within different cultures and people work to achieve these needs in accordance with the customs of their own societies.

If you live in a tribal village in Outer Mongolia, the acquisition of another yak may give you added social status. In most Western societies, the equivalent would be a large house or an expensive car. For example, having a Mercedes can be a way of satisfying the need for self-esteem since it can indicate an individual's position in society. For others, it could be achieved by a more prestigious job title.

Expressions of social status are important to people and are powerful motivators once the physiological drives are satisfied.

People will also work better for incentives such as a prize holiday for being top salesman. This is not just because the prize in itself is enjoyable, but because winning it clearly indicates an individual's achievement compared with that of his or her colleagues. For some this makes the effort worthwhile.

Level 3: Personal Ambitions

Neither basic requirements nor social status tell the whole story – neither are entirely sufficient. The third and most powerful driving force is to satisfy personal ambitions.

People want to develop themselves and do better at their chosen occupation. This means setting individual objectives which can enhance personal development, and working towards their achievement.

Often there is no apparent rhyme nor reason why someone seeks a certain goal, or is determined to achieve a specific objective. These individual ambitions are usually related to something that has captured the imagination or in which a talent has been demonstrated. People tend to work hard at things they are good at.

The desire to achieve personal aspirations is a powerful motivator and is a continuous process. It never ceases because as soon as one ambition is achieved, another usually presents itself. The need to realize an ambition is a far more compelling force than is often recognized.

Motivating Effects

The three primary needs – basic requirements, social status and personal ambitions – can be operating at the same time. The higher needs are extremely influential, but they are meaningless if the other lower needs are not satisfied.

If, for example, the need to achieve personal ambition is frustrated, an increase in the other levels of need may well take place. So it is useful to recognize the following:

- Once a basic need has been satisfied, there will be an instant desire to satisfy those needs which have yet to be satisfied.

- The less a particular need is satisfied, the more important it becomes.

- The less a higher level need is satisfied, the greater the importance a lower level one will assume.

If people cannot get what they want, such as the ability to develop their skills, they will demand more of what they can get. Hence, the demand for more money may be hiding a desire for a more challenging job, or a hankering for perks may be masking a need to be appreciated by others.

Summary: Understanding Needs

There are basic drives which everyone seeks to satisfy. Together these form the mainspring of human behaviour.

Unless lower order needs are satisfied, motivation is impossible. The fulfilment of these needs takes away dissatisfaction and prevents people feeling disgruntled about their lot. It does not necessarily motivate people to improve their productivity.

Having an understanding of people's basic needs is essential, for without this knowledge you cannot start to appreciate what motivating is all about.

Questions to Ask Yourself

Think about the basic needs people have, and ask yourself the following questions:

♦ Do I understand the driving forces which people require to satisfy?

♦ Do I understand the part that money plays in satisfying these drives?

♦ Do I understand the social needs which people desire to be fulfilled?

♦ Do I understand the individual nature of personal ambition?

♦ Do I understand that the satisfaction of basic needs does not necessarily motivate people to improve their performance?

♦ If people ask for more to satisfy a lower level need, could this be because their higher level needs are not being met?

You Will Be Doing Better If...

★ You understand the various levels of driving forces which people require to satisfy.

★ You understand the part that money can play in satisfying these drives.

★ You understand that the less one of the basic needs is satisfied, the more importance it assumes.

★ You understand that the satisfaction of basic needs does not necessarily motivate people to improve their performance.

3.   Designing the Work

Understanding the needs that people require to be satisfied is one thing. Understanding what motivates people to work well is another thing altogether. To get people to want to work to their fullest potential means ensuring that the right conditions are created and that what they are doing is a source of satisfaction, something they think is worth doing.

To do this you need to understand how work can be designed to provide people with the best possible level of job satisfaction.

Doing Something Worthwhile

People who lack motivation are often viewed as being lazy, with the assumption that lazy people usually lack motivation. This is not true. More often than not, the cause of dissatisfaction is not the job itself, but the conditions in which it is done.

For example, a person will read a novel in one sitting, but will get bored after twenty minutes when studying a textbook. Or, someone will find pressing buttons repetitive and tedious when working on an assembly line, but will spend hours performing precisely the same action on a slot machine in the local amusement arcade. It is not the activity which produces demotivation or boredom, it is the content or the situation in which it is being carried out. If people do not achieve satisfying outcomes from their activities, they perceive this as tedious and useless.

Creating the Right Conditions

When people are asked to indicate what they like and dislike about their work, the aspects they say they like are usually significantly different from the ones they dislike. They are rarely the direct opposite of each other.

For example, people usually feel good about:

- Being skilled at doing the work itself.
- Achieving a high standard.
- Having their efforts recognized.

These are intrinsic aspects which relate directly to making a specific effort and are under the personal control of the individual. Whereas, the sorts of things people feel dissatisfied about are:

- Company policy and methods.
- Red tape and bureaucracy.
- Working conditions.

These are external or extrinsic features of work, things over which most people have little control.

22

What is more, if the causes of dissatisfaction are eliminated, motivation to do better does not automatically ensue.

For people to be motivated, you need to ensure they are given the opportunities to carry out those activities which they find rewarding, and that they are protected from those things that may interfere with the completion of their tasks.

Providing Satisfaction

For people to give their best to their work, they need to have pride in it and to gain pleasure from it. In order for work to provide satisfaction, people need to:

- **Perceive the work as meaningful**. If the job appears to be important and interesting, they are more likely to feel motivated.

- **Be made accountable for the results of the work**. If people view the quality of work they do as dependant upon their personal effort rather than upon outside factors, they will tend to feel more proud of the outcomes; they will be more concerned to ensure that the work is up to standard.

- **Be given feedback on performance.** If people regularly find out how they are performing, they will feel good and be stimulated to do better.

It is worth looking at these three factors – work content, accountability and feedback – in more detail in order to identify what you need to do to provide as many of these 'job satisfying' conditions as possible.

1. Perceiving the Work as Meaningful

For people to feel that what they are doing is meaningful, the work needs to be of a high quality. This means:

- **Having different things to do**. Doing the same, limited task all the time is soul-destroying. People are likely to consider that what they are doing is worthwhile if they carry out a variety of activities which develop their abilities.

- **Completing the whole task**. Doing it all rather than only a small part, or seeing something through to the finish. It is satisfying to be able to say, "I did that" or "I made this". Being shown the end product may also help to engender this feeling.

- **Producing or doing something worthwhile**. Doing something which is of assistance to others or making something useful enables people to feel helpful and significant.

To analyse the work that people do you need to consult them. This enables you to find out if their work is providing them with the variety and range of activities which brings them satisfaction. It gives them the chance to let you know if reorganizing their tasks would provide them with a better quality of work.

2. Being Made Accountable

For people to feel good about their work the right level of autonomy needs to be provided and fostered. This means:

- **Allowing freedom**. Instead of giving orders, offer people the discretion to carry out and schedule their tasks. This encourages them to devise their own methods and makes them readier and happier to take responsibility.

- **Giving power**. Instead of making all the decisions, make people accountable for the results of their work. This allows them to take personal pride in what they are doing.

It is important that you give people the opportunity to take on responsibility. By becoming more involved in their work they will be far more willing to be held to account for results.

Therefore you need to establish which individuals would like to be made more responsible in one way or another. This often produces surprising results. For instance, an assistant who worked a strict 9-5

25

day and who was thought to be uninterested in the work, was discovered to be thoroughly frustrated by lack of responsibility and yearning to take on more; and when given it, worked round the clock.

Shouldering desired responsibility is a great motivator; so is taking on extra responsibilities, provided you make it clear to people that this is a way they can develop themselves, and you take an obvious interest in their progress.

The more you can provide the conditions for individuals to feel they manage their own destiny at work, the more involved they will feel, and the more prepared they will be to make the extra efforts required to achieve a successful outcome.

3. Being Given Feedback

For people to perform better they need to receive feedback about how they are doing. This means:

- **Agreeing clear and attainable standards**. This provides people with a yardstick against which to measure their performance, and allows them to get feedback for themselves from their own experience.

- **Having regular reviews**. This allows people to communicate their problems and discuss methods of improving performance.

Telling people how well they are performing, and indicating in a sympathetic and constructive way where improvement might be made, provides them with the motive to do better. You can do this by:

- Seeing them on a regular basis.
- Discussing their performance and agreeing where they are doing well as well as where they would be able to do better.
- Finding out what else they would like to do, and what they would like someone else to do.
- Agreeing the methods and facilities for doing so.
- Following up the results of those ideas and confirming that any improvements made are having the desired effect.
- Being constructive when critical.
- Praising when performance is good.

In this way people learn where they require to do better as well as being motivated to carry on good work where they are already doing well.

Summary: Being Satisfied

It is important that you do all you can to ensure that the right conditions are present for motivating people to work well.

For work to give satisfaction, people must feel that they are doing something worthwhile. They also need to know the importance of their work and to be allowed to complete as much of the whole task as possible.

Taking responsibility enables them to take control of what they are doing, and to feel that they are making a positive contribution.

Knowing how well they are achieving their work provides them with the encouragement to keep doing what they are doing well, and directs their attention to those tasks they could do better.

The more meaningful you can make the work, the more interest people will take in what they are doing. The more freedom you allow people, the more they will be prepared to be accountable for the results. The more you let them know how well they are functioning, the more personal satisfaction they will get from doing the job itself.

Together these conditions create a solid foundation for people to work better and to make an extra effort.

Questions to Ask Yourself

Think about the work that people are required to carry out and answer the following questions:

♦ Are people being given the opportunity to do those things which come under their personal control?

♦ Do they perceive their work as worthwhile?

♦ Do they have a variety of tasks to do?

♦ Are they able to see a task through to completion, or at least see the end product?

♦ Are they being offered responsibility?

♦ Are they being provided with feedback on how well they are doing?

♦ Are constructive suggestions being given for those areas that need improving?

♦ Is everything being done that can be done to ensure the best possible conditions for people to achieve satisfaction from their work?

You Will Be Doing Better If...

★ You ensure that people are doing the things which they control.

★ You know what people enjoy about their work and discuss how things can be improved in areas they find frustrating.

★ You ensure that they know what is significant about what they do.

★ You let them do as much as possible of the whole task.

★ You enable them to be as responsible as they wish to be.

★ You provide regular feedback on performance.

★ You are doing everything you can to apply the right conditions for satisfactory work to take place.

4. Inspiring Performance

Motivating people to want to achieve results means inspiring them to want to do well. To encourage people to do better at their work, and be more creative, you have to set up a suitable climate for them to want to make an extra effort. The amount of trouble you take to create the right environment is directly related to the level of performance you inspire.

Ensuring Competence

An underlying pre-condition to inspiring performance is making sure that people are able to carry out their activities competently. Competent people are far more confident in their abilities and more motivated.

Any changes to their work pattern, or any additional responsibilities may alter an individual's level of competence. And the requirement to develop new skills may mean that some people are no longer as capable as they once were.

Some of the signs to notice which indicate that people lack competence, are frustration, loss of confidence and reluctance to accept responsibility. If this is the case, you need to identify the areas where people are not performing to standard (or are unsure of their ability) and help them acquire the appropriate skills.

There are several simple ways of doing this:

- Some kind of external formal training experience which will provide both theory and practice, such as courses for a day or a week, etc.

- In-house training which will enable practical, specific skills to be learned. For example, sitting at 'Nellie's elbow', provided that Nellie has both the appropriate expertise and a constructive attitude.

- One-to-one coaching which will provide expertise that is tailored to specific needs. This may be expensive but because it can be precisely focussed, it tends to be the most cost effective.

If these methods to improve performance can also contribute to a recognized qualification, it provides another incentive to do well. Make sure that after people have undergone training you review their progress and give praise for work well done. By helping people to perform better you show that you are interested in them, which in itself is motivating.

Accommodating Individual Needs

Tailoring work to meet individual needs shows people that they are valued. This can easily be done by:

- Enabling people to work flexi-time or core time (e.g. a 24 hour week or 10.00-4.00 each day) or have the option to work part-time when it suits them better. Identify the various options available to individuals. If two people are to share a job, ensure that duties are agreed and hand-overs are worked out.

- Permitting essential personal telephone calls; for example, to check on child-minding arrangements. A pay-phone could be installed for the purpose, which would inhibit the number of calls to members of the family in Australia.

- Allowing time during working hours for important personal appointments such as visits to the dentist, doctor, parent/teacher meetings, etc. Agree times and dates of such visits so that you are able to arrange for jobs to be covered as required.

- Encouraging opportunities to socialize; for example, by arranging a Christmas party or negotiating a discount for the membership of a local gymnasium; Better still, obtain suggestions from people themselves and encourage those who are most interested to organize the activities.

Allowing individuals to work in a way which suits them means they feel they are appreciated in their work.

Relieving people of unnecessary stress and worry in their personal lives should enable them to give their full attention to their work. Encouraging them to get to know each other better forms more productive working relationships.

Providing Incentives

The provision of incentives is based on the premise that people will increase their efforts when they are given a specific reward or encouragement for good performance. But incentives only work if :

● The reward on offer is perceived as worth having and worth making an extra effort for.

● The additional performance can be measured objectively and directly accredited to individual achievement.

● The increased level of performance does not become the new minimum standard.

If the first two conditions do not apply, receiving an incentive will be considered to be a nice extra, but will not necessarily cause people to perform more productively. If the third condition is violated, the incentive will cease to be regarded as a motivator. For example, if an extra effort is required for a rush job, everyone may be quite happy to give up half an hour at lunchtime in return for half a day off when the job is completed. But if people subsequently find that from then on they are expected to take less time for lunch this would cause them to become disillusioned and less willing to make an extra effort next time.

If incentives are to produce the desired results, you need to work out what sort of reward would be effective in motivating people. So discuss this with the people concerned and make sure the promised reward is forthcoming when the target is achieved.

Praising Positively

People value being praised when they have performed well. If they have put in an extra effort, receiving praise for a job well done makes their extra effort worthwhile.

The way to do this is by:

- Recognizing the situation in which people should be praised instead of letting good work slide by without notice or without calling attention to it.

- Making time to say "Well done" rather than throwing thanks over your shoulder on your way out.

- Giving unconditional praise.

It is important to give unconditional praise ("That is/was brilliant.") because if you praise and criticize in the same breath, e.g. "You did that very well, but..." you will get the reputation for being a 'but' person, someone who is never pleased.

Many people mistakenly believe that they can use praise for the bit which is right, to sweeten the unsatisfactory bit. But those receiving criticism will only remember the criticism and not the praise. This will have the effect of demotivating them instead of motivating them and reduced levels of performance will almost certainly result.

However, when there is a justifiable need to criticize, by all means do so. Then, when the task is completed to the right standard, give the praise that is due.

The point is to make sure you do these things on entirely separate occasions, even if they are only ten minutes apart. This way your praise will achieve its positive and motivating effect.

Summary: Stimulating Motivation

To stimulate motivation you need to make sure people are competent, and that you accommodate their individual needs where possible, provide appropriate incentives and, above all, praise them. This way, you inspire people to want to perform well.

Questions to Ask Yourself

Think about how you ensure that people are motivated and answer the following questions:

♦ Are people fully competent in the tasks they are required to perform?

♦ Are those who were competent suddenly exhibiting signs of incompetence?

♦ Have I explored various training options for restoring and/or improving levels of performance?

♦ Have I looked at the possibility of tailoring work to fit individual needs?

♦ Do people consider the incentives offered are worth working for?

♦ Do I praise people whole-heartedly when they have achieved something?

♦ Am I certain that I do not mingle criticism with praise?

♦ Do I praise people enough?

You Will Be Doing Better If...

★ You encourage people to make their own decisions.

★ You offer extra responsibility to those who want to develop further.

★ You make sure that they are capable of carrying out their tasks.

★ You understand the conditions under which incentives could be productive.

★ You are prepared to adapt the work to fit in with individual needs wherever possible.

★ You provide extra facilities which will assist people in managing their outside responsibilities better.

★ You give constructive criticism.

★ You make sure that any criticism of performance is given on an entirely separate occasion from any praise given for performance.

★ You praise people for their efforts.

5. Maintaining Motivation

Once people are performing in a highly-motivated way, it is important to work at maintaining their momentum. This is done by keeping a watchful eye on standards and morale. If you do not notice when things fall below standard, people will think you do not care. And if you do not sense when morale is low, things could rapidly deteriorate. Both are essential concerns for maintaining high levels of motivation.

There are several practical ways of keeping morale at a high level.

Keeping People Informed

The more people know about what is happening, the more confident they are about their work and this has a positive impact on maintaining morale. Keeping people informed does not mean telling them about plans which are confidential. It simply means ensuring that the information people are given is as correct and as up-do-date as that which is available to you. You can do this by:

- Keeping yourself informed about what is going on.
- Letting people know as soon as you do.
- Explaining how the information could affect them.

A lack of knowledge usually lowers morale and, therefore, motivation, so make sure that you pass on information accurately and immediately, preferably in person.

Maintaining Performance

Once motivation is present, like the oil that keeps the cogs turning in a machine, you need to ensure that standards of performance are constantly topped up. There are three basic ways of doing this:

- A regular maintenance.
- A major overhaul when required.
- A review at agreed intervals.

For these activities to be effective, you need to carry them out in a positive and encouraging way.

Day-to-day Maintenance

No matter how motivated people are, they need to know that their efforts are being appreciated. They will also value being advised when they could do something better before it becomes a major problem. It is demoralizing to be told that something has not been done properly for some time when calling attention to it earlier would have made all the difference.

This means you need to keep a watchful eye on what is going on to ensure that things are running smoothly and that you make minor adjustments when they are required. You can do this by:

- Showing concern for people themselves and not just for their work.
- Encouraging discussion about how their work is going and giving practical advice when appropriate.
- Pointing out where minor improvements need to be made and discussing what could be done.

People like to feel that what they are doing is being noticed and that they are playing a valuable part.

Major Overhaul

Sometimes, no matter how hard you work to motivate people and encourage them to achieve what is required, their performance is well below standard and it is obvious that they are not motivated. It is easy to assume that this is due to reluctance or a poor attitude. The temptation is to express exasperation or annoyance "How many times have I told her...?" "He never does what he's supposed to" without realizing the demotivating effect this can have on other people within earshot. Rather than reacting antagonistically, showing irritation or getting angry, you need to control your feelings and plan a course of action:

- Identify the precise area or areas where a gap has occurred between existing performance and the expected standards of performance.
- Fix a time to see the individual privately and ensure that no-one else can overhear.
- Find out why performance is below standard.
- Agree a course of action for improvement.

You must also make it clear that you want this person to succeed and that you will be giving him or her as much help and encouragement as you can.

Performance Review

Day-to-day maintenance and the occasional overhaul keep things ticking over but do not necessarily indicate that things are on target. To check this, you need to carry out a periodic performance review, rather like an MOT test for cars to ensure they are roadworthy. This helps people to see how they are progressing and gives them the impetus to carry on the good work.

The topics to discuss are:

- **Past performance**. What a person feels he/she has achieved and what could have been done better.
- **Future activities or plans**. What is likely to happen and what part the person would play in this.
- **Objectives**. What additional responsibilities the

person might take on.

A periodic review gives people an overall sense of direction, a feeling that they know where they are going. It forms a reference point to return to if things become fraught.

All these ways of reviewing performance help to maintain motivation by keeping people on track and enabling them to focus clearly on what they are trying to achieve.

Controlling Influences

Individual personalities can influence levels of morale. How this is controlled or harnessed is important if confidence is to be maintained.

Occasionally you may find there is someone who affects others for the worse. It only needs one rotten apple in the barrel for the others to be contaminated at frightening speed. A negative attitude that is too ingrained to change may undermine all your efforts and possibly place the business itself in jeopardy. It may mean that you have to part company with this person because he or she is a bad influence, no matter how excellent their ability to do the job.

Motivated people have a positive effect. If you put a

ripe tomato among green tomatoes it will ripen them more rapidly. So it is with people. If there is someone who is positive and enthusiastic, these energies will soon affect the others. If you can use this dynamism to advantage, you will find that maintaining morale is a great deal easier.

Improving Surroundings

People tend to work better in pleasant working conditions. The surroundings do not in themselves create motivated people, but they can prevent people from becoming unnecessarily dissatisfied.

Making the workplace more agreeable need not involve a major redesign. It can be done by, for example:

- Giving the walls a lick of paint from time to time to prevent them from becoming shabby. Newly decorated premises lift people's spirits and give them a fresh start.

- Choosing objects in primary colours, such as red, green and yellow, which keep people cheerful.

- Providing people with individual coffee mugs which makes them feel wanted.

- Having a decent rest area with newspapers and specialized trade magazines which people would not necessarily buy themselves gives them the opportunity to gain further insights into the business or professional world in which they work and keeps them abreast of developments.

- Installing a soft drinks and/or coffee machine so that people have the freedom to manage their breaks without wasting time.

- Making facilities for food available (especially if you are located off the beaten track). This eliminates the inconvenience of going out for sandwiches or having to bring individual provisions to work.

- Improving the existing lighting. This can have a dramatic effect on the atmosphere and prevent people from becoming tired and irritable.

All these things are positive ways of maintaining performance and letting people know they are appreciated.

Although there may be some cost involved in providing such facilities and surroundings, the amount of goodwill and the extra effort that is generated usually far outweighs, as well as repays, the additional expense.

Summary: Sustaining Effort

Keeping a high level of motivation requires as much effort as achieving motivation in the first place.

Making sure people know what is happening inhibits non-productive rumours and enables them to concentrate on getting the work done.

People need to be clear about how well they are doing their work and corrective action has to be taken when this is required. A periodic overall review allows people to take stock and reminds them how they fit into the bigger picture.

Providing a pleasant environment indicates to people that they are valued and makes the work more congenial. This makes it easier to sustain the effort to produce the required results.

Maintaining morale requires that you keep alert for signs of demotivation. By detecting any changes in levels of enthusiasm, appropriate action can be taken to restore and sustain optimum levels of performance.

Questions to Ask Yourself

Think about whether you are working positively to sustain people's motivation and answer the following questions:

♦ Do I keep people informed promptly about things which affect them?

♦ Do I take an interest in people?

♦ Do I help people to rectify their mistakes?

♦ Do I keep a watchful eye on performance and work to redress poor performance promptly?

♦ Do I help people to review their performance and make action plans for their future development?

♦ Do I provide the most pleasant surroundings for work that I possibly can?

You Will Be Doing Better If...

★ You make sure that people get information promptly.

★ You know how they are performing in their work.

★ You identify the areas where performance is not up to standard and take steps to correct it.

★ You help them to put together an action plan for their future development.

★ You use other people's enthusiasm to maintain morale.

★ You make surroundings as pleasant as you can within your financial limits.

★ You are always prepared to help people do better.

6. Your Attitude to Motivating

Your attitude is as important when motivating people as theirs is, because how people behave will be mirrored to a considerable extent by your attitude.

Having a Positive Outlook

If you allow things to get on top of you, you may become demotivated and unwittingly communicate this to others through your behaviour. This in turn will affect their performance adversely. If you behave in a positive way, this will act as a catalyst to others.

By making the work both challenging and fulfilling, people will be motivated to contribute their best.

You can demonstrate your positive outlook by:

- Being enthusiastic about the work in hand.
- Encouraging people in their work.
- Being willing to help out when required.
- Letting people know you are committed to achieving the task.
- Listening to what people have to say.

Enthusiasm is an essential personal quality in motivating others. You need to remind yourself constantly to:

- See the good rather than the bad.
- Believe whole-heartedly in the overall aims.
- Communicate your beliefs and values clearly.

If you do not allow setbacks to detract from your determination to achieve objectives and you refuse to take 'No' for an answer, you will be seen as someone who never gives up. This encourages others to behave in the same way.

Your positive outlook influences other people to follow your example. And the more you can help people to be enthusiastic about doing things, the more highly motivated they will be.

Showing Interest

If you can let people know that you are interested in what they are doing, it stimulates them to get things done. When asking individuals to do something for you, try to put it in a way which indicates that you understand what motivates them. "I know you enjoy doing this, and I'd be glad if you could get it done by Tuesday."

This is important if you want to ensure they will work hard instead of just turning up.

To show interest, you need to know:

- The particular ambitions of each individual so that you can delegate the right quality of work.

- The skills people would like to acquire, so that you can offer them the opportunity to develop.

By asking interested questions you can identify the different things that motivate different people. You will soon realize that what motivates one person will not necessarily motivate someone else. This allows you to offer the right opportunities to the right people.

Behaving Consistently

Since others take their cue from how you behave, it is important that you behave consistently. This enables people to know where they stand with you, and have the confidence to predict how you will react in most circumstances. Behaving consistently means:

- Being sure enough of your objectives that you do not make spontaneous decisions which could upset the status quo.

- Counting to six before reacting, so that you have a chance to work out a more considered response.

- Staying calm in all circumstances, whatever the provocation, so that people know you are in control.

51

If your moods are unpredictable, people cannot be sure of the reception they will get and so will tend not to admit their problems. A consistent level of behaviour reassures them and gives them the confidence to share their concerns.

Keeping up the Good Work

You know when you are doing the right things because people respond positively and are more productive.

However, on rare occasions, even though you are doing everything you should, someone does not respond. The important thing to realize is that if you are doing everything you should be doing, the problem does not rest with you but with that individual.

You should endeavour to find out what is causing an individual's lack of motivation to see if there is anything you can do to improve the situation. But if the problem is so deep-rooted that whatever you do never improves the situation, you either have to live with it or get rid of the cause.

Try not to let such an experience affect your attitude even though it is natural to dwell on the casualties rather than the successes. A failure with one person or in one situation should not prevent you from trying again in similar circumstances because no one person will behave in exactly the same way as another. Remind yourself that for every person who does not respond there are many that will – or at least enough to make all your efforts worthwhile.

Summary: Motivating Attitudes

When you understand the underlying forces and factors to motivating, it is apparent that there is no magic formula which will instantly create motivated people.

It is your attitude and subsequent behaviour which is the key – not only to motivating people in the first place, but keeping them motivated once you have.

It is important that you fully realize how powerful an influence you can be in the whole process. So make sure that you take as positive an approach as possible.

Questions to Ask Yourself

Think about your attitudes to motivating and answer the following questions:

♦ Do I work to keep a positive attitude despite everything?

♦ Am I always willing to help when required?

♦ Do I strive to see the good rather than the bad?

♦ Do I let people know that I am always interested in what they are doing and how they are getting on?

♦ Do I work at being even-tempered and approachable in all circumstances?

♦ Am I aware of how my behaviour will directly affect others' morale and motivation?

♦ Am I fully committed to motivating people no matter how demanding this may prove?

You Will Be Doing Better If...

★ Your attitude to motivating is positive.

★ You show a genuine interest in other people's work and help them to do better.

★ You keep your equilibrium in all circumstances.

★ You know how your behaviour can influence the morale and motivation of others.

★ You work to keep a high level of enthusiasm and communicate this appropriately.

★ You always look for the positive rather than the negative.

★ You never give up motivating people, even if it may not work all the time.

Check List for Motivating

If you are finding that motivating others is proving more difficult than you thought, think about whether this is because you could have failed to take account of one or more of the following aspects:

Understanding Individual Needs

If people do not respond, it may be because you have not fully understood that the driving forces merely get people out of bed to come to work. It could be that you are offering the wrong things to motivate them. You may also be underestimating their abilities and not providing them with the right opportunities to work to their capacity.

Making the Job Fit

If people complain that their work is mundane and boring, it may be that you need to examine the job in detail to see if improvements can be made. Finding out what they would like to do and consulting with them as to how they think the work could be done will help you do this. By enabling people to take on more responsibility, and providing them with constructive feedback, they are likely to produce better quality work. In this way you involve them and enhance their motivation.

Inspiring People to do Better

If you find that performance does not seem to be improving, it may be that you have not fully appreciated your role in encouraging others. You need to find the courage to let people take responsibility and do the work in their own way. Allowing people more control makes them want to work harder. Recognizing good work and praising it keeps people wanting to do better.

Maintaining Performance

If you find that people's performance is falling off, it may be that you are not keeping up the momentum. You may not be visible enough or are not communicating directly with people so that they are unsure of what is expected of them or what is happening. Being available to assist and advise as necessary keeps people focussed and ensures they feel involved. Taking some care over working conditions makes the place a pleasant one to work in and indicates that people are valued.

Generating Enthusiasm

If people get the impression you are not interested, it is hardly surprising if they are not motivated. You may have to indicate more clearly that you want them to enjoy what they are doing and that you care not only about the quality of work they produce but also about them as individuals.

The Benefits of Motivating

Motivating people means understanding what drives and stimulates people to work well. It is achieved through a combination of understanding their individual needs and creating the opportunities for them to want to work well.

The benefits of working with motivated people are that:

- Work will be done to the right standard and within the designated time-scales.

- People will enjoy doing the work and feel valuable.

- People will work hard because they want to do what they are doing.

- Performance will be monitored by the individuals concerned and will not require much supervision.

- Morale will be high, which provides an excellent working atmosphere all round.

Once people are motivated, sustaining their momentum requires constant vigilance, but the effort is well worthwhile. The simple and powerful truth is that highly motivated people will perform well and achieve results.

Glossary

Here are some definitions relating to Motivating.

Achieving – Excelling in the attainment of a goal by hard work and effort.

Autonomy – Having the freedom and discretion to schedule work and determine the procedures used when carrying it out.

Competence – The ability to do the job.

Driving forces – The needs that get people out of bed, but do not necessarily motivate them to work better.

Frustration – The difference between expectation and achievement.

Feedback – Reaction to performance which, if communicated correctly, increases performance.

Hierarchy of needs – A pecking order of needs, the satisfaction of some of which bring others to the fore that still require to be satisfied.

Incentive – Enough enticement to incite action.

Job satisfaction – A thorough fulfilment from work.

Morale – A confident attitude of mind demonstrated by positive behaviour and an optimistic outlook.

Motivation – The willingness to exert high levels of effort towards a goal, provided the effort made also satisfies some individual need.

Need – The difference between a desired state and the actual state.

Objectives – Direction for effort.

Performance – Dramatic production.

Praise – Warm approbation which encourages people to carry on the good work; a much under-used motivating activity.

Responsibility – Being given the power to make decisions and take control.

Reward – Award for all the effort.

Motivating Theories

A number of theories relating to motivation are regularly mentioned. Here are some of the better-known ones.

Maslow's hierarchy of needs theory – The theory that individuals have five needs – a need for survival, for security, for social intercourse, for self esteem, and for fulfilment of potential; and that, as each need is satisfied, the next becomes more dominant.

Alderfer's ERG theory – The theory that there are three core needs: existence, relatedness and growth.

Herzberg's motivation-hygiene theory – The theory that intrinsic factors, such as responsibility, recognition and achievement are related to job satisfaction, while extrinsic factors, such as pay and working conditions, are associated with dissatisfaction.

McClelland's theory of needs – The theory that achievement, power and affiliation are the three important needs required for motivation.

Vroom's expectancy theory – The theory that acting in a certain way depends upon the strength of the expectation that the act will be followed by a given outcome, always provided the outcome is attractive enough to warrant the effort.

The Author

Kate Keenan is a Chartered Occupational Psychologist with degrees in affiliated subjects (B.Sc., M.Phil.) and a number of qualifications in others.

She founded Keenan Research, an industrial psychology consultancy, in 1978. The work of the consultancy is fundamentally concerned with helping people to achieve their potential and make a better job of their management.

By devising work programmes for companies she enables them to target and remedy their managerial problems – from personnel selection and individual assessment to team building and attitude surveys. She believes in giving priority to training the managers to institute their own programmes, so that their company resources are developed and expanded.

Having long believed the key to successful motivation is about being positive and encouraging others, she admits to finding it something of an effort to remain constantly motivated herself. She is rewarded by the fact that no-one else seems to suspect that any effort is required.

THE MANAGEMENT GUIDES

	Book £2.99	Tape £4.99
Asserting Yourself	☐	
Communicating*	☐	☐
Delegating*	☐	☐
Handling Stress	☐	
Making Time*	☐	☐
Managing*	☐	☐
Managing Yourself*	☐	☐
Motivating*	☐	☐
Negotiating*	☐	☐
Planning*	☐	☐
Running Meetings*	☐	☐
Selecting People*	☐	☐
Solving Problems*	☐	☐
Understanding Behaviour*	☐	☐

Just tick the titles you require and send a cheque or postal order for the value of the book to: B.B.C.S., P.O. Box 941, HULL HU1 3VQ (24 hour Telephone Credit Card Line: 01482 224626). Add for postage & packing (in the UK) £1.00 for the first book & 50p for each extra book up to a maximum of £2.50. Overseas (& Eire) Orders: £2.00 for the first book, £1.00 for the second & 50p for each additional book.

*These books are also available on audio tape. Telephone 0800 435 067, or send a cheque or postal order for the value of the tape to: Sound FX Publishing, P.O. Box 3246, Chelmsford CM2 8WZ, and add for postage & packing the same amount as specified for book postage above.